UNCLE OLLIE'S ALPHABET FOLLIES
written and illustrated by
Dugg Smith

for Annabelle and Elias
my partners in rhyme

Archway Publishing books may be ordered through booksellers or by contacting:

Archway Publishing
1663 Liberty Drive
Bloomington, IN 47403
www.archwaypublishing.com
844-669-3957

ISBN: 978-1-6657-1174-6 (sc)
ISBN: 978-1-6657-1173-9 (e)

Print information available on the last page.

Archway Publishing rev. date: 11/03/2021

HELLO! I AM UNCLE OLLIE

I was working on my alphabet the other day, right over there

but it seems to have slipped away somewhere...

Oh...I see it under the chair.

A spider named Walter lives here too, way up by the ceiling

or on the lamp...wherever he wants to actually...

away from the mouse who also lives in the house but under the chair.

I see the alphabet is moving along the floor.

Alphabets usually stay where you put them.

They usually begin with A and go on from there but;

Oh--You'll get the hang of it. Let's begin...

 **is for Aardvark.**

Well why not?

The Aardvark has a great long snout
Where Ants go in and can't get out
Another name for snout is nose
ill bet his hurts him when he blows

A pig-like thing that hunts at night
He doesn't even need a light
To find his food. He sniffs it in
Then heads back home to wash his chin

A is also for Ants

Finding ants isn't hard
They're in the house and in the yard
Running left then running right
I wonder where they sleep at night?
I'll ask the Aardvark he's sure to know.

I guess that I don't mind the ants
I just don't like them in my pants

 **is for Bear**

But this bear isn't bare
It has lots of hair
Something's wrong there.

Another bear who isnt bare is
A polar bear
A polar bear has soft white hair
To keep him warm
Because, Where he lives
there is no heat
And no galoshes for his feet.

If it gets too long
he can go to the Barbear
with the comfortable chair
and leave some there.

B is also for Bandicoot
But that's another poem altogether.

 **is for**

Camel

A Camel has a hump (or two)
Depends on where he's from
He mostly lives in deserts
with lots of sand and sun

He can drink a hundred litres
in a quick 10 minute slurp,
walk around for many days
and never need to burp

The Camel's name means beautiful
I think that just depends
on If you're a camel
Or perhaps, a camel's mother.

is for Dung Beetle

He has an awful life.

Unless he takes a lot of baths

He'll never get a wife.

E is for **Elephant**

Elephants are very large

But you shouldn't call them chubby

They never forget, you know,

And you could wake up with a bed full of

peanut shells or straw

(or maybe something even more ugghy).

 is for Frog

A frog can sit on a log in a bog.
Or on a pad in a pond or
under a frond in the rain.

If he falls in the water, he won't drown.
He's an excellent swimmer and will just go
round and round.

He can sit where he wants and
wait for bugs to fly down
to his tongue that can stretch across the street
when he sees the fat bug that he wants to eat.

(F is also for Fly, BTW)

 is for Goose

Is a goose loose?
I haven't a clue
Is a goose silly?
no more so than you

Can a goose be goosed?
I suppose so; I can't really say
but Gooses are useful in dozens of ways

We get goosebumps and goose
eggs, goosenecks and gooseflesh
We have goosegrass, goose grease
gooseberries and even goose steppers
lately, I've thought about planting
goose peppers.

With so many uses
if they all flew away
it would cook all our gooses
the very next day

H is for HIPPO...POTTO...MUSS

HIPPOPOTOMUS?

That's a very long name.

And being very large is the Hippo's claim to fame.

But he likes little things too

like the bugs that cling to his skin

and the birds that eat them.

is for Iguana

An Iguana doesn't wanna. Do you?

Iguanas are kind of ugly and look like dinosaurs

With rough skin and spiky things all over the place

Even on their face.

They can disappear into the bushes

and when you don't expect it; whack you with their tail

which is long and strong and can fall off

and grow right back again.

K is for

Kangaroo (and Koala, too)*
Both are from 'Down Under'
where they roam quite free

One on the ground
and one in a tree
usually.

K

*could also be for

Knight

This knight doesn't like to fight
he would rather play with his Kite
at night...with no light
in the park after dark
...What a lark!

Hark!

Wait just a minute!

What happened to J?
It seems to have run away.
Let's just put it here. It'll stay.
And I know what it should say.

 is for Jaguar

"He who kills with one leap"
named by the Indians because they'd
seen him kill with one bite.
His jaws will cut through anything,
crocodiles, turtles, Impalas, and even GTOs.

He swims well, climbs quickly, attacks from the water,
the trees, or the open plain.
he's fast and powerful as a train.

Logging has cut his habitat in half
So his family now lives in rainforests and
wetlands in Brazil.
He's not extinct. He's with us still.

L

is for llama

A llama has too many L's
I wonder why that is?
He is very like a camel,
which is another kind of mammal
But with a sensible number of L's.

I once met a llama's mamma.
She seemed to be quite nice.
Yes, I met a llama's mamma.
In fact, I met her twice.

is for Monkey

A monkey climbed up in a tree
To look down on folks
And see what he could see

When he was up so high
Near the sky like that
he felt that he could almost fly;
But he couldn't.

so instead, he peed
on someone's hat!

Monkeys are like that, you see.

N is for

Nyala

A Nyala is a South African Antelope

who looks quite regal indeed

With large curved gold-tipped horns

And markings like no animal has ever worn;

Zebra-like stripes, a crown of golden hair,

a long handsome beard, and golden boots upon his feet.

A beautiful sight If you happen to see him roaming about

But he's timid; so you won't likely find him hanging out

He eats fruit and grasses and prefers

to graze early in the morning or late at night

at watering holes where he can get plenty to drink

but stay out of sight.

 **is for**

Owl

or Otter or Osprey or Oriole or Ostrich

(Oddly, they are all birds, except for the otter,

which isn't –- A bird that is.)

The Owl comes out at night

because of his sight, which is good-very good.

He likes to hang out where it's dark in the woods.

He says, whoooo?

And if someone answers, he kills them.

(That isn't true. Don't listen to me.

I like to scare people Fiddle-dee-dee)

O is for Ostrich

The Ostrich is the
most giant bird in the world
He cannot fly,
but he can sure run fast.

He sticks his head
in the sand;
but not to hide.
just to make sure
the eggs haven't died.

# P is for Penguin

He's the funniest guy
in his fancy suit and tie
He shuffles along in the cold
Or goes for a swim to catch fish for his kids.

Some Penguins don't mind cold;
And some don't mind hot
But all of them swim really well,
As for flying—
Alas, they cannot.

is for Quayle

Dan Quayle.

He used to be vice president

of the United States

Google it.

You can ask him for a potatoe if you wish.

R **is for Rabbit,**

Rabbits don't really live in top hats
and pop out when magicians want them.
Rabbits live in fields and woods, and gardens
and have names like Peter and Flopsy and
steal carrots and things
from friendly farmers everywhere.
They are cute, though!

 **is for Sloth**

he's lazy as hell
He Hangs all day from the trees
by his tail
Sleeping and sleeping
Until he feels like a swim
Then drops in the water on a whim
to paddle a bit
Till he gets tired and decides to quit
Then sleeps again for a few hours or days

Ah, what a life!
He loves to just laze.

T is for Troll

I met a troll the other day
while walking home from school
he said hello
we talked a while. I told him he was cool.

I asked if he could walk me home
so we could talk some more.
He said he could and did
right up to my front door.

He said his name was Carl
I thought that rather odd
but I took his hand and shook real hard
and told him I was Todd.

I asked If he could come inside
and meet my mom and sis
if they don't see you with their eyes
they never will believe this

OK, said Carl, Let's go inside
I can even stay to eat
but whatever else we do
don't let them see my feet

my feet are green and hairy
with bumps and warts and twigs
with uncut nails and scratches
and worms I've tried to squash

If your mother's like the others
she'll try to make me wash.

U is for Umbrella

An umbrella is not an animal
but it's very useful in the rain
or even in the strong sun

Fighting with an umbrella
on a windy day is never any fun
You'd be tempted to say it IS an animal
and consider tossing it down the drain!

Ah, but then you'd get wet
and your hat would blow away
so, hold that umbrella tightly,
don't let if fly away today
Wait till tomorrow, then smash the nasty thing!

V is for Vulture

A vulture is a bird of prey; he likes to eat dead stuff.

He doesn't kill them by himself - but waits for someone else to do it.

He hasnt got the strength it takes, but he is good at waiting.

He sits or flies way up high enjoying the 'scent of the crime'

until it looks to him like it's HIS dinner time.

Other animals wont eat him because he isn't very picky

he'll eat anything dead even if they have diseases.

His stomach is immune so he doesnt get all icky.

if he thinks an owl is nearby.

far away he will quickly fly.

is for Walrus

You can tell that it's a walrus because it has
a big moustache, large tusks, and flippy-floppy feet.
His favorite meal is "all you can eat"
...clams
Sitting on an Ice shelf, he'll eat 4000 clams
by sucking out the meat and spitting out the shells
back into the sea, with a very hearty splash.
(but not in the trash like he should)

He can dive down deep to find his clams
or swim away as fast as your car across the icy waters.

X is for Xenarthran

If he looks like a monster- just let me say
He's a leftover creature from dinosaur days.

A 3-banded Armadillo lives in swamps and eats lots of bugs.
I get the feeling he doesn't want any hugs.

His families are Sloths and Anteaters too.
They have one thing in common:
They like eating bugs alone in the dark
not at a picnic in a lovely park.

Y is for Yak

Can you Yack with a Yak?
Maybe.
if you help him put his pack on his back,
he may even yack back

He's known as the 'boat of Tibet."
If you've something to haul
The yak's who you call.
He'll carry it all
And won't get upset.

He eats only grass and weeds
and can breathe the thin air with never a care
That good old Yak will take you anywhere
and bring you back!

Z is for Zebra

–of course, it is

Why wouldn't it be?

A dazzle of Zebras is something to see

He looks like a horse, or maybe a donkey

But you surely cant ride him, so don't even try

He's simply not tameable.

He's not that kind of guy.

His family's called a harem.

His stripes are all white;

They keep away insects who are trying to bite.

He's a magical beast,

quite a visual feast!

But you can only look and see,

don't touch him,

he wants to stay free!

Well Mates

I think we've gone as far as we can

with this alphabet thing.

There are no more letters.

But that's ok.

I have many stories to tell you someday.

So watch for

"Uncle Ollie Tells Short Tales"

Coming Soon!

Printed in the United States
by Baker & Taylor Publisher Services